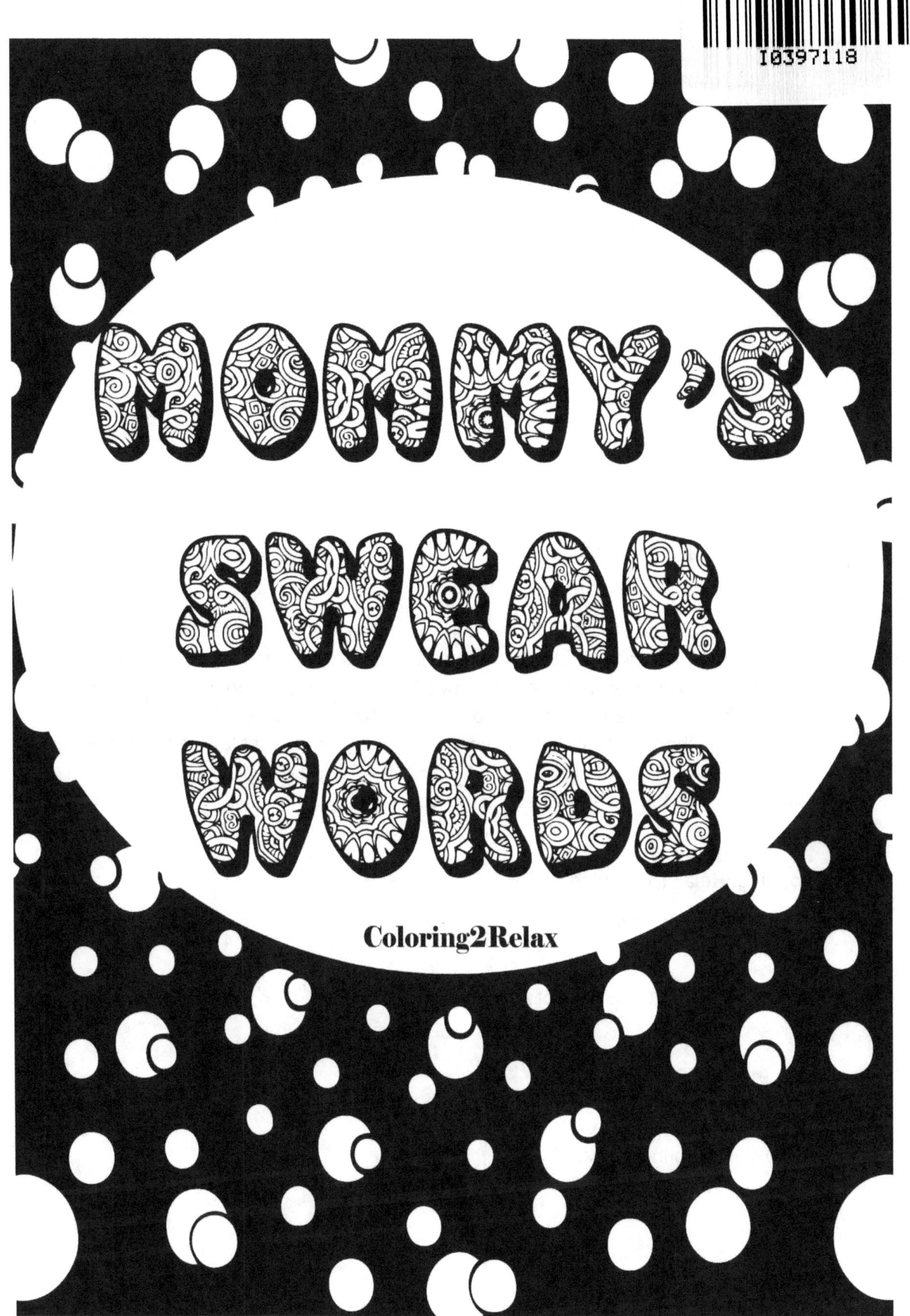

Copyright © 2017 by Coloring2Relax

All rights reserved. No part of this publication may be reproduced, distributed or transmitted in any form or by any means, including photocopying, recording or any other electronic or mechanical methods, without the prior written permission of the publisher, except in the case of brief quotations embodied in critical reviews and certain other noncommercial uses permitted by copyright law. For permission requests, contact the publisher, with "Attention: Permissions Coordinator" in the subject field, at the email address listed below.

Coloring2Relax Publishing

support@coloring2relax.com

Printed in the United States of America

First Printing, 2017

http://www.coloring2relax.com

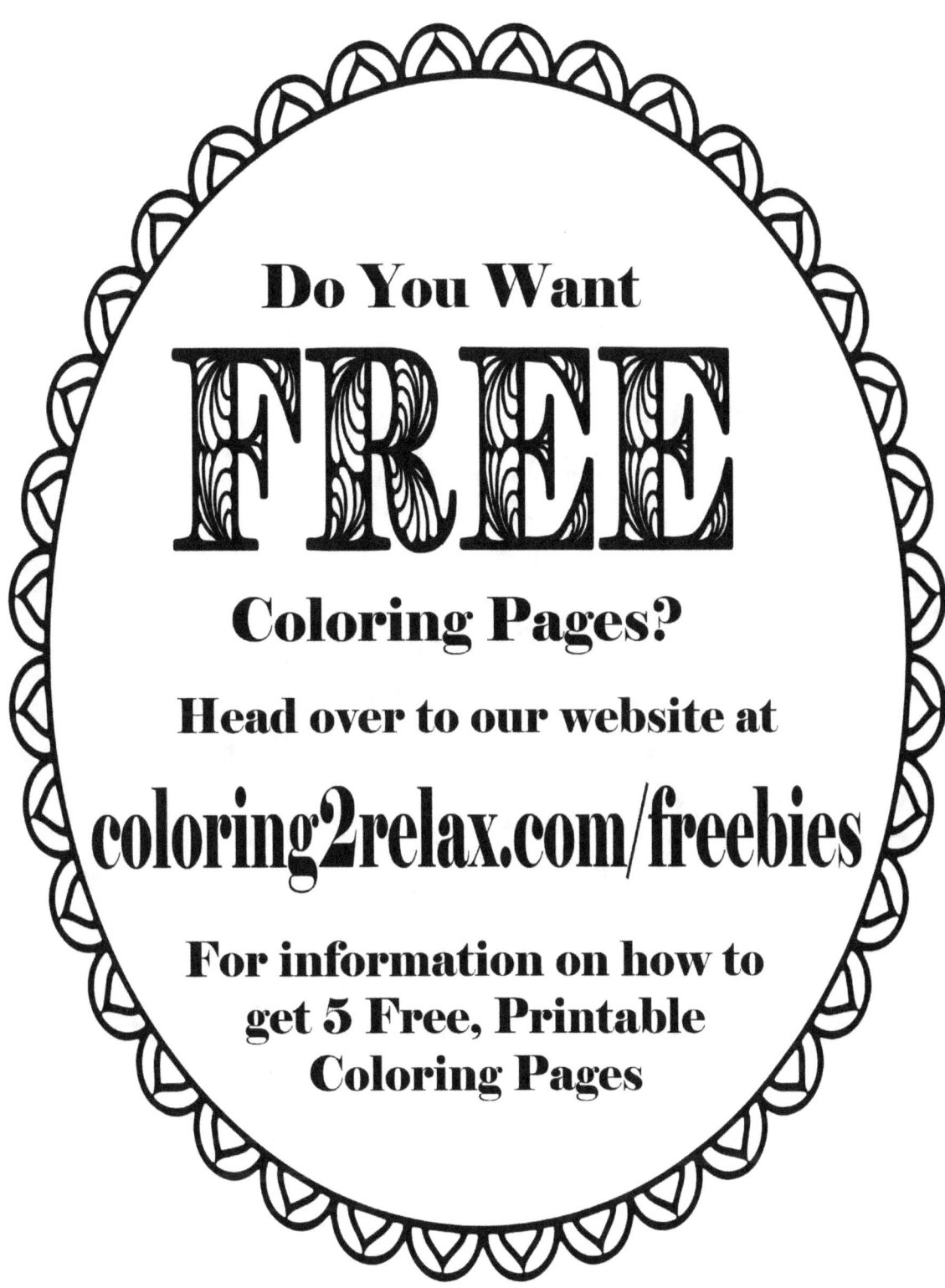

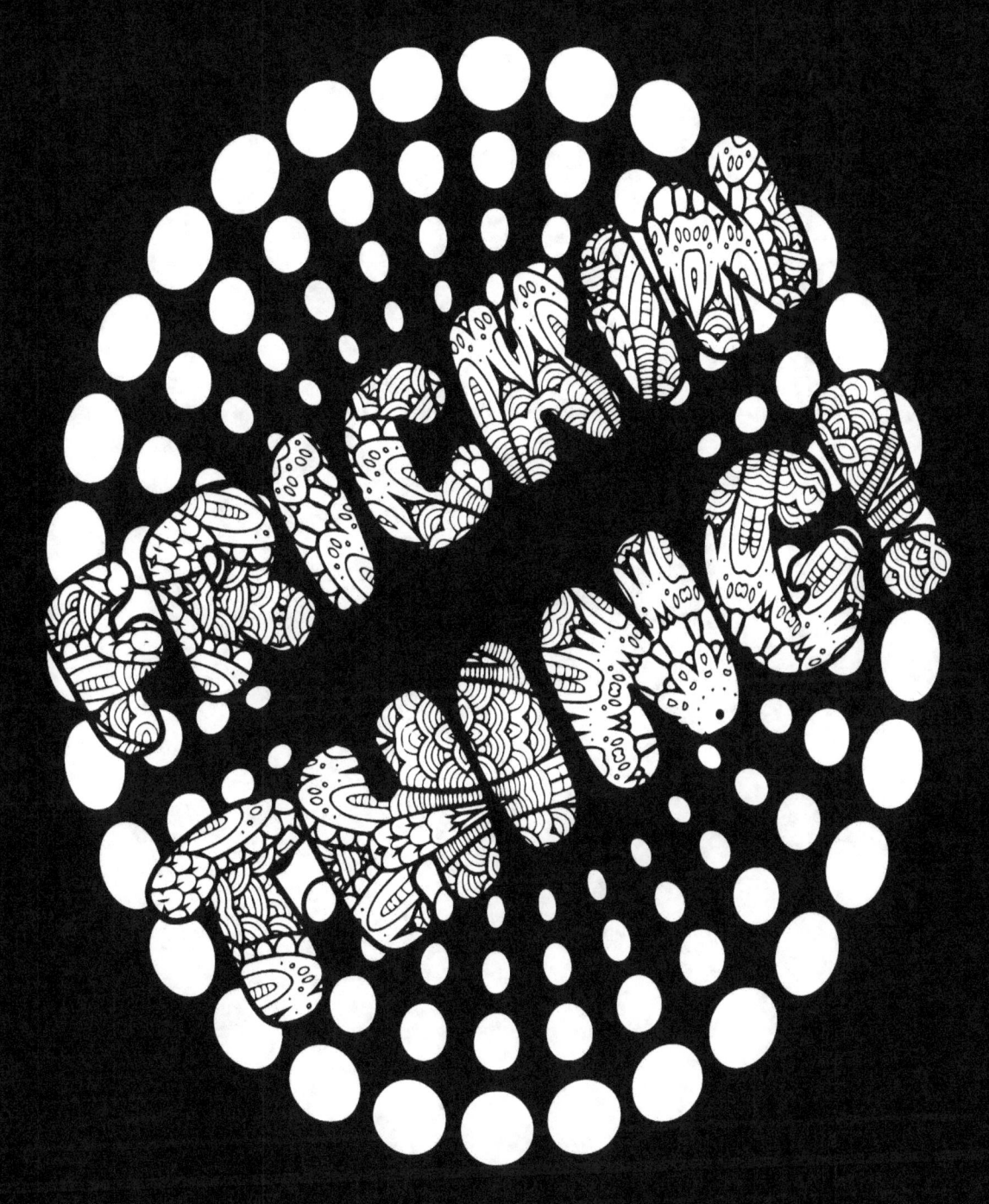

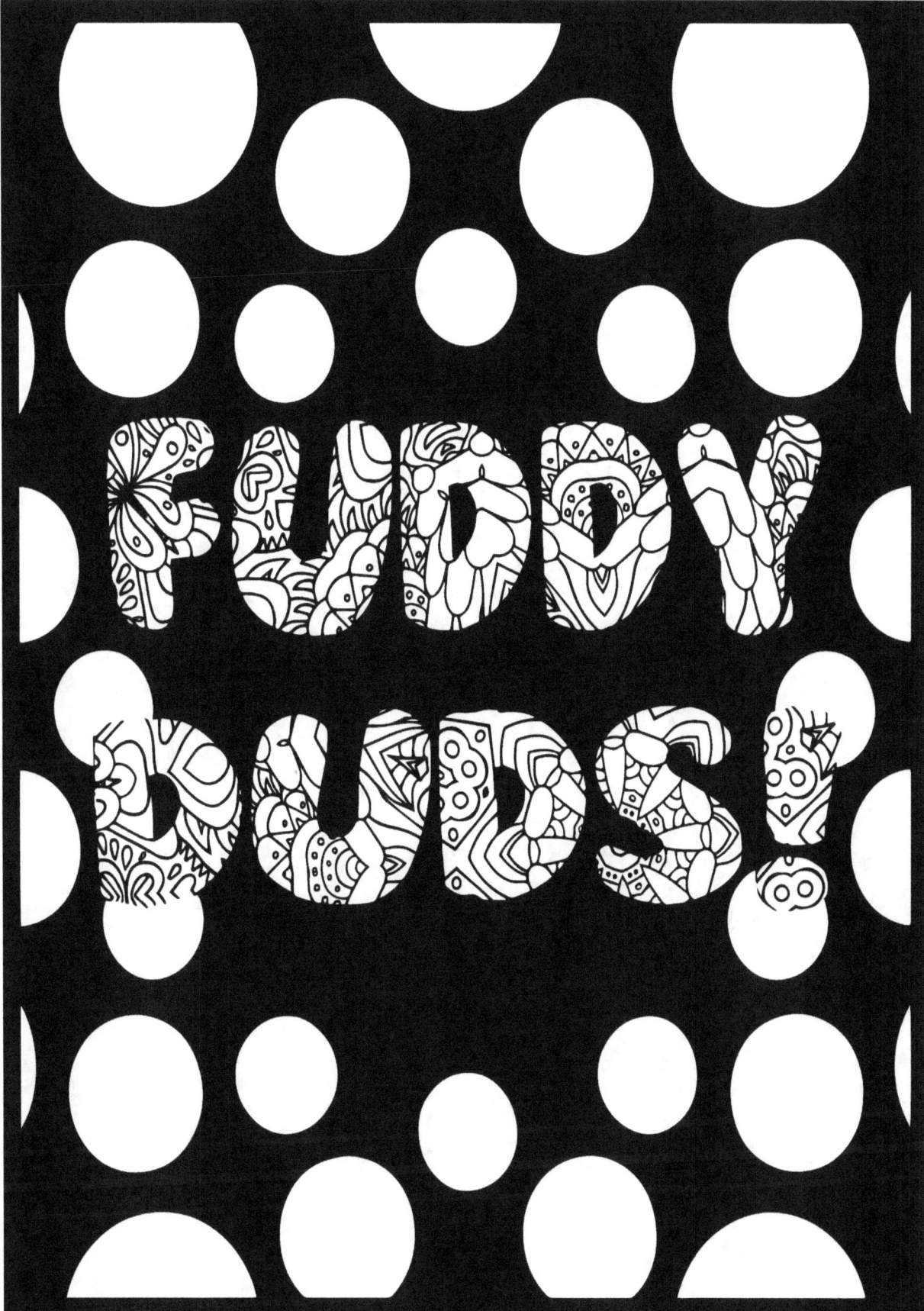

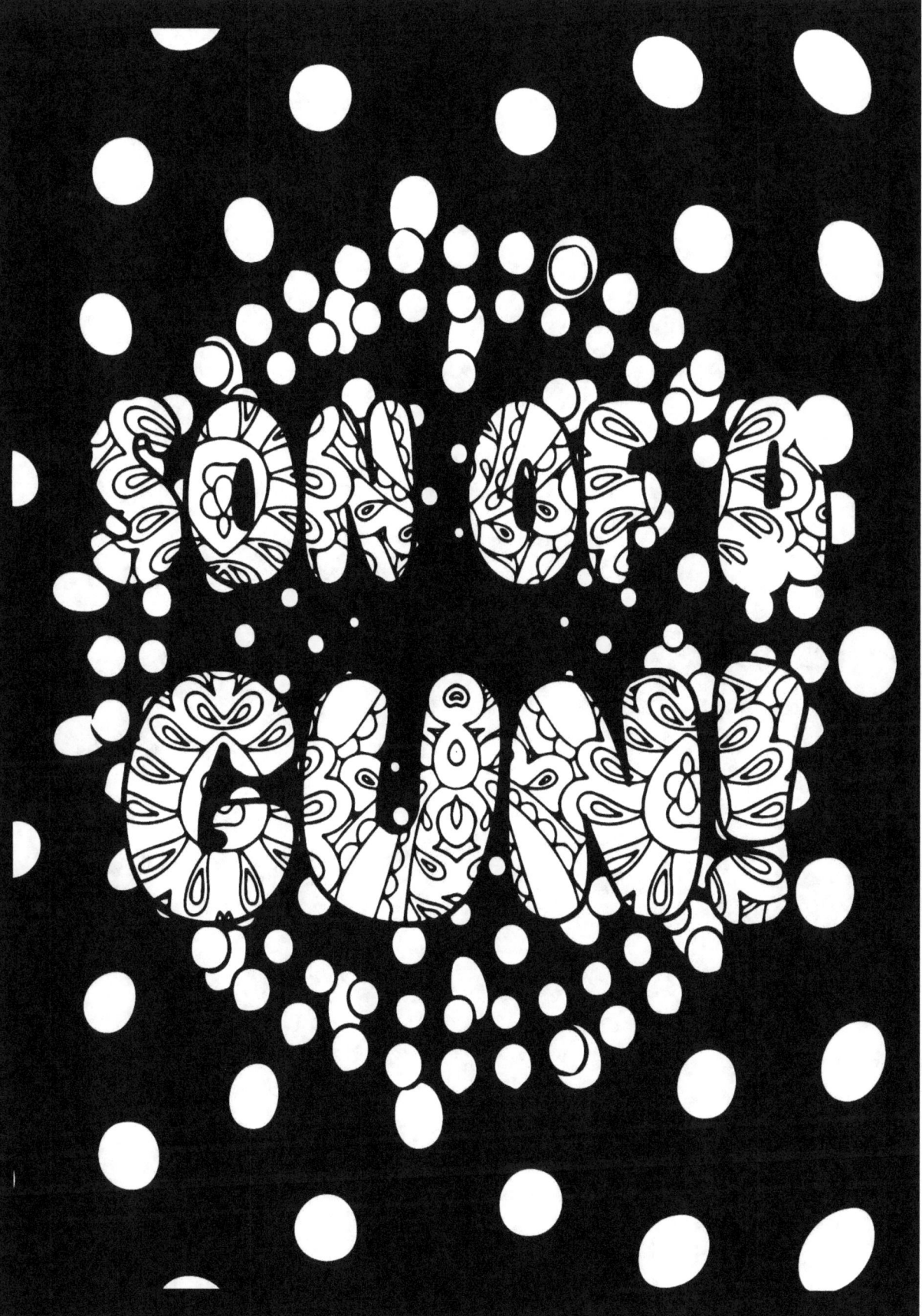

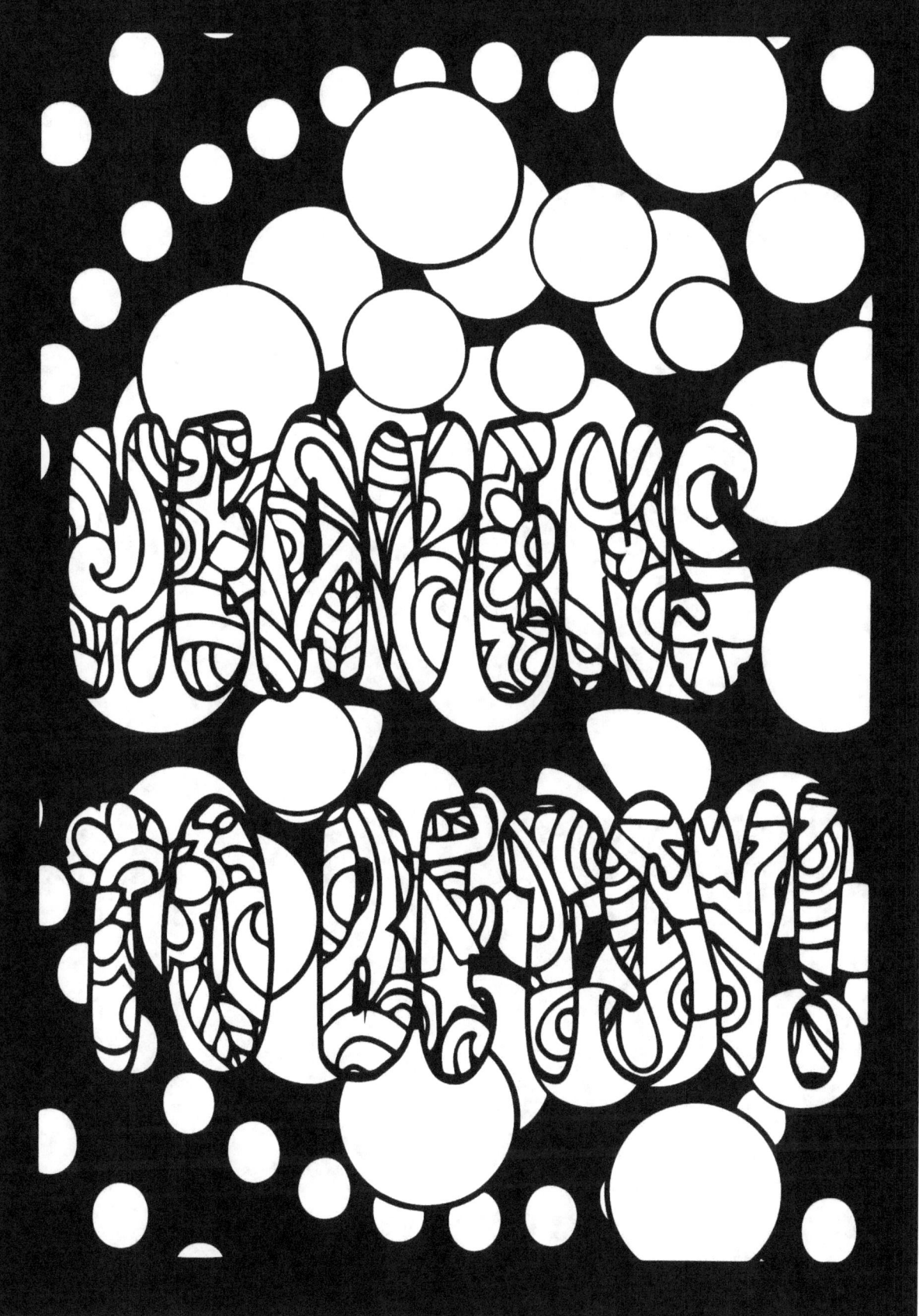

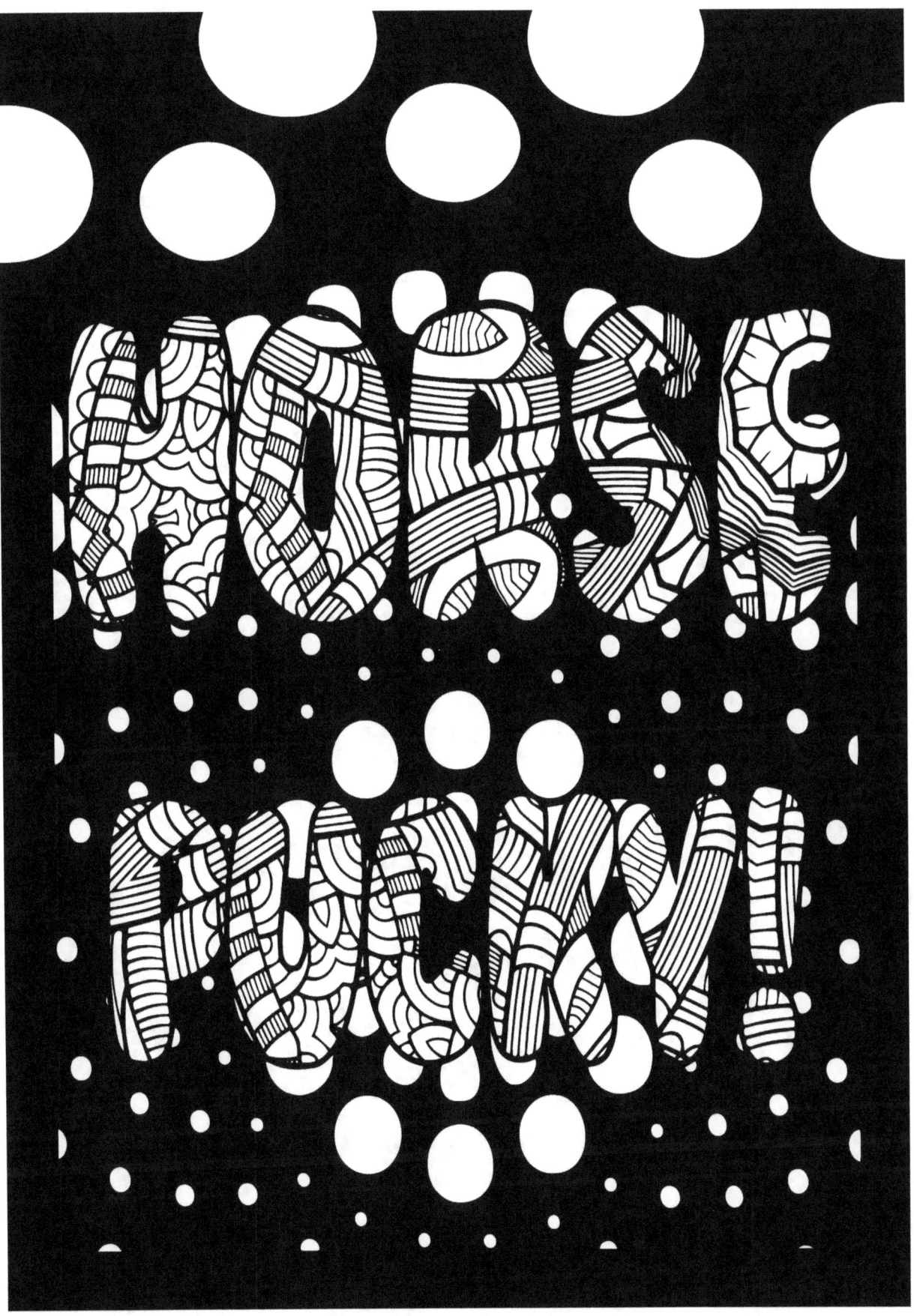

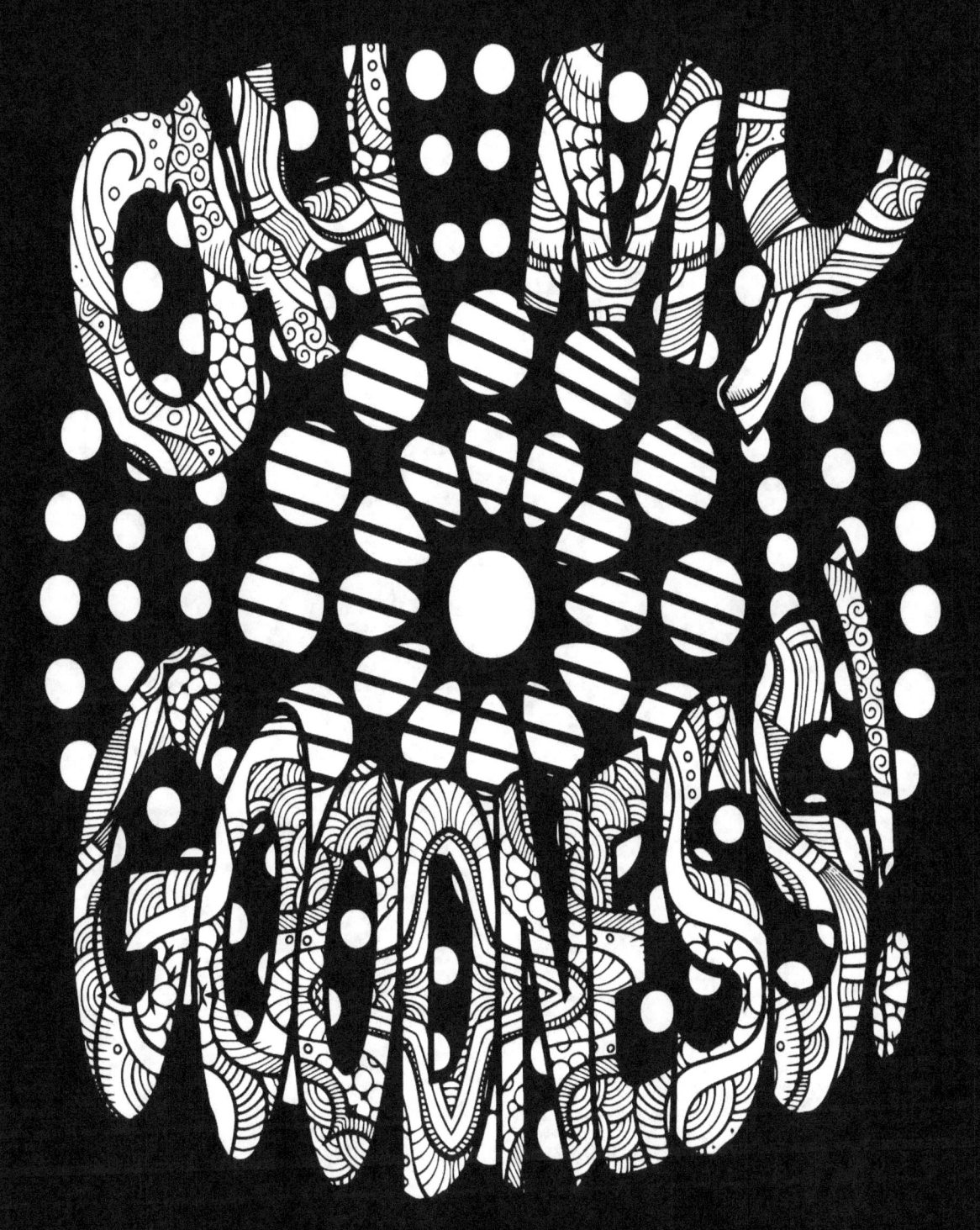

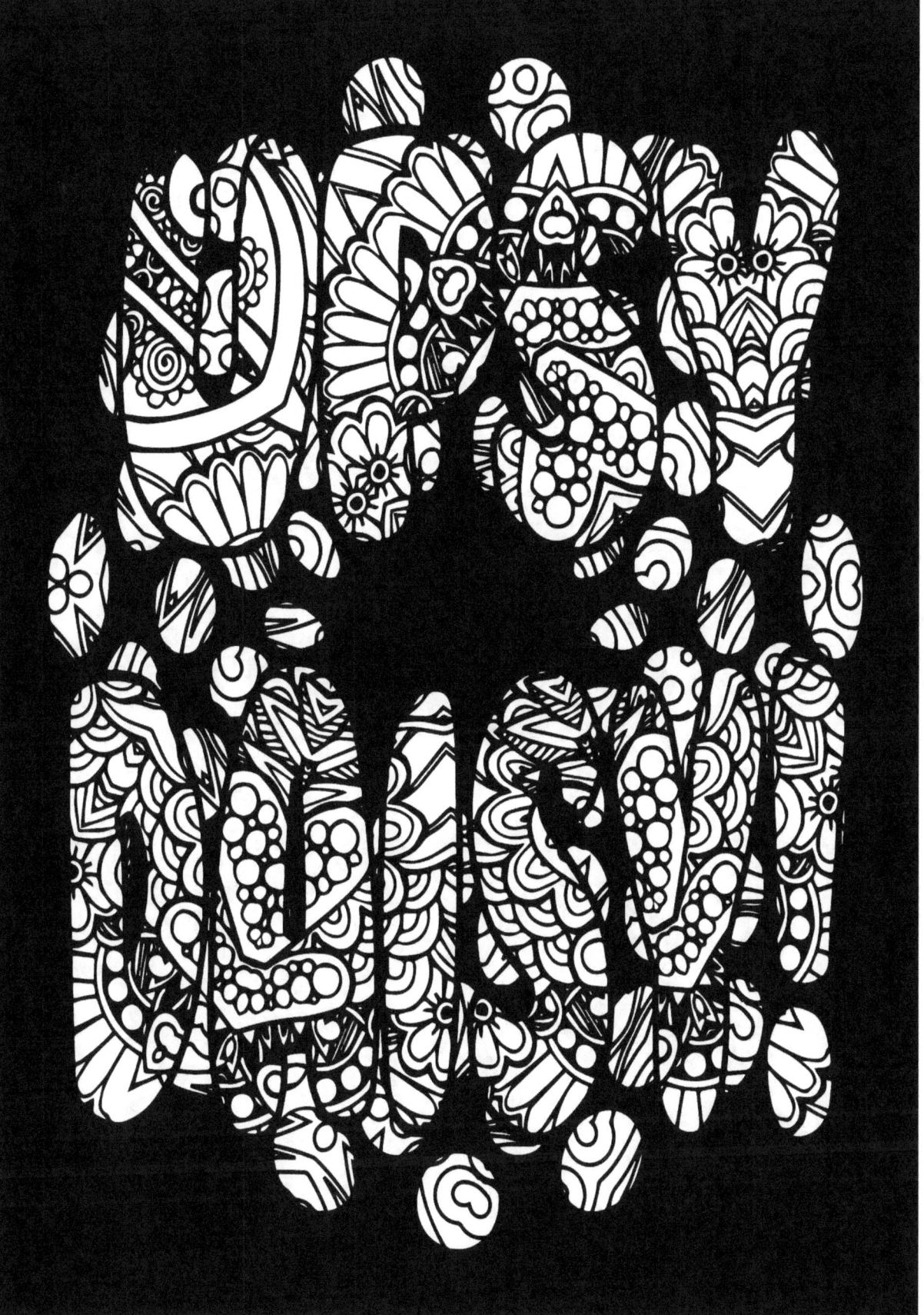

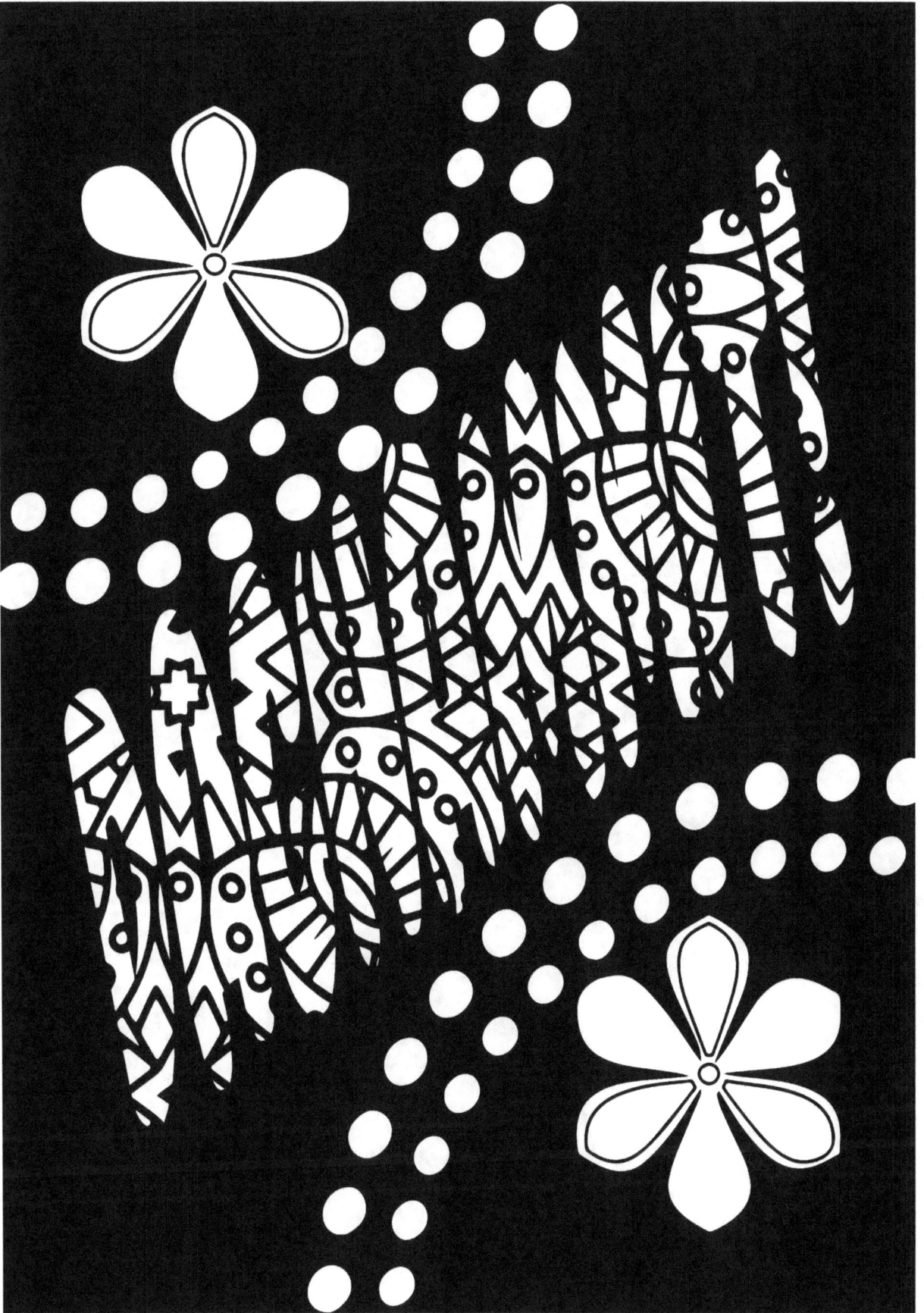

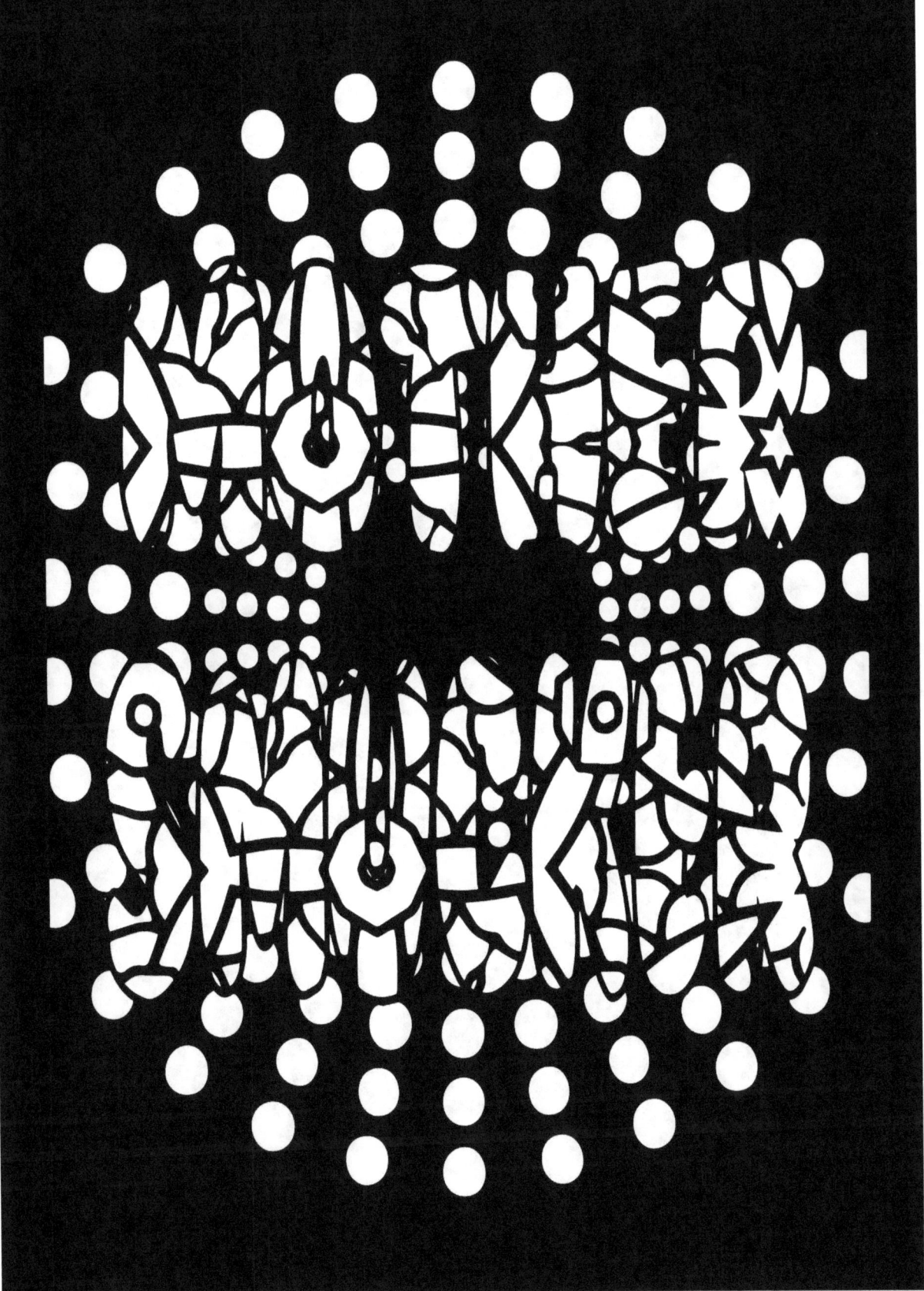

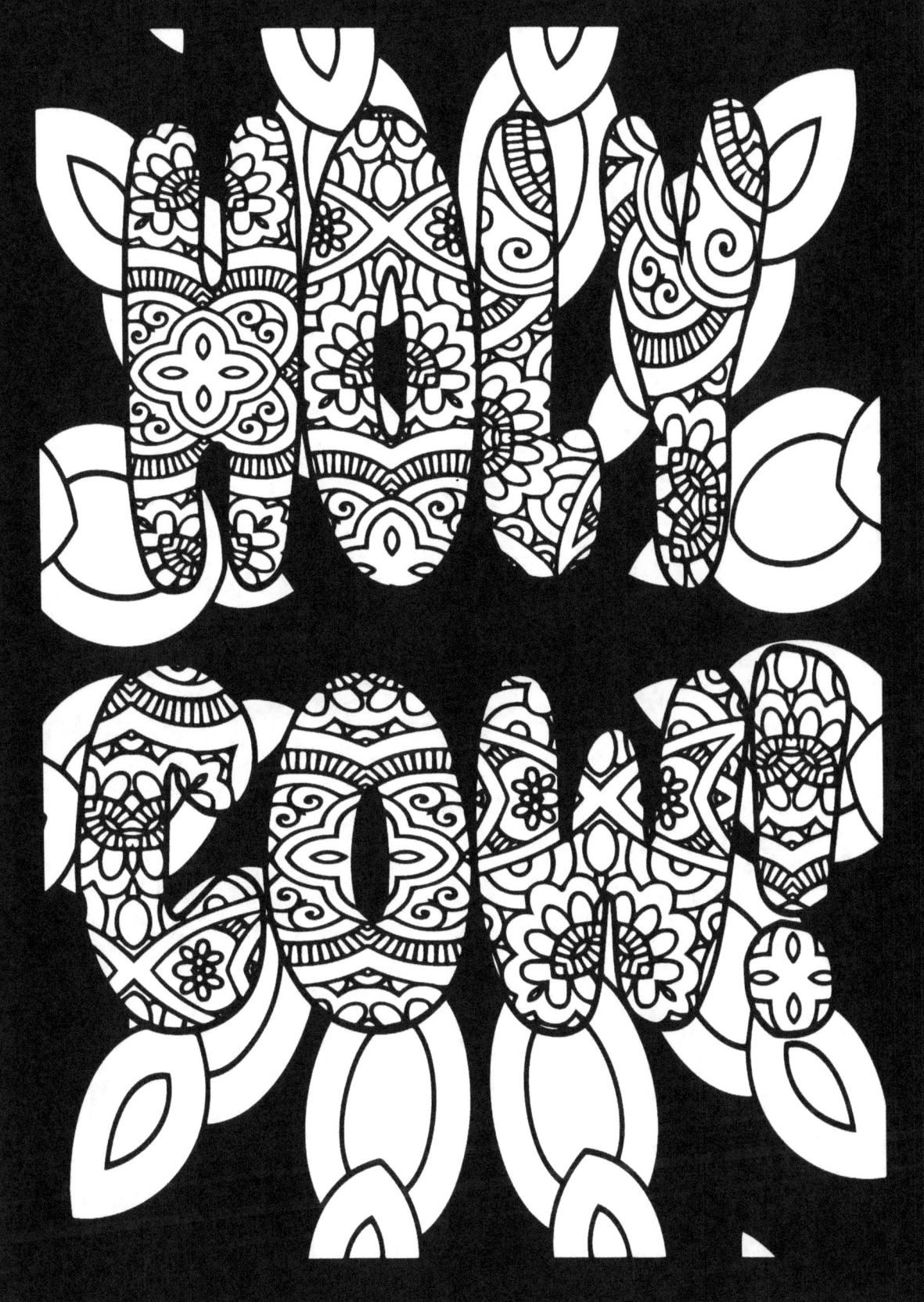

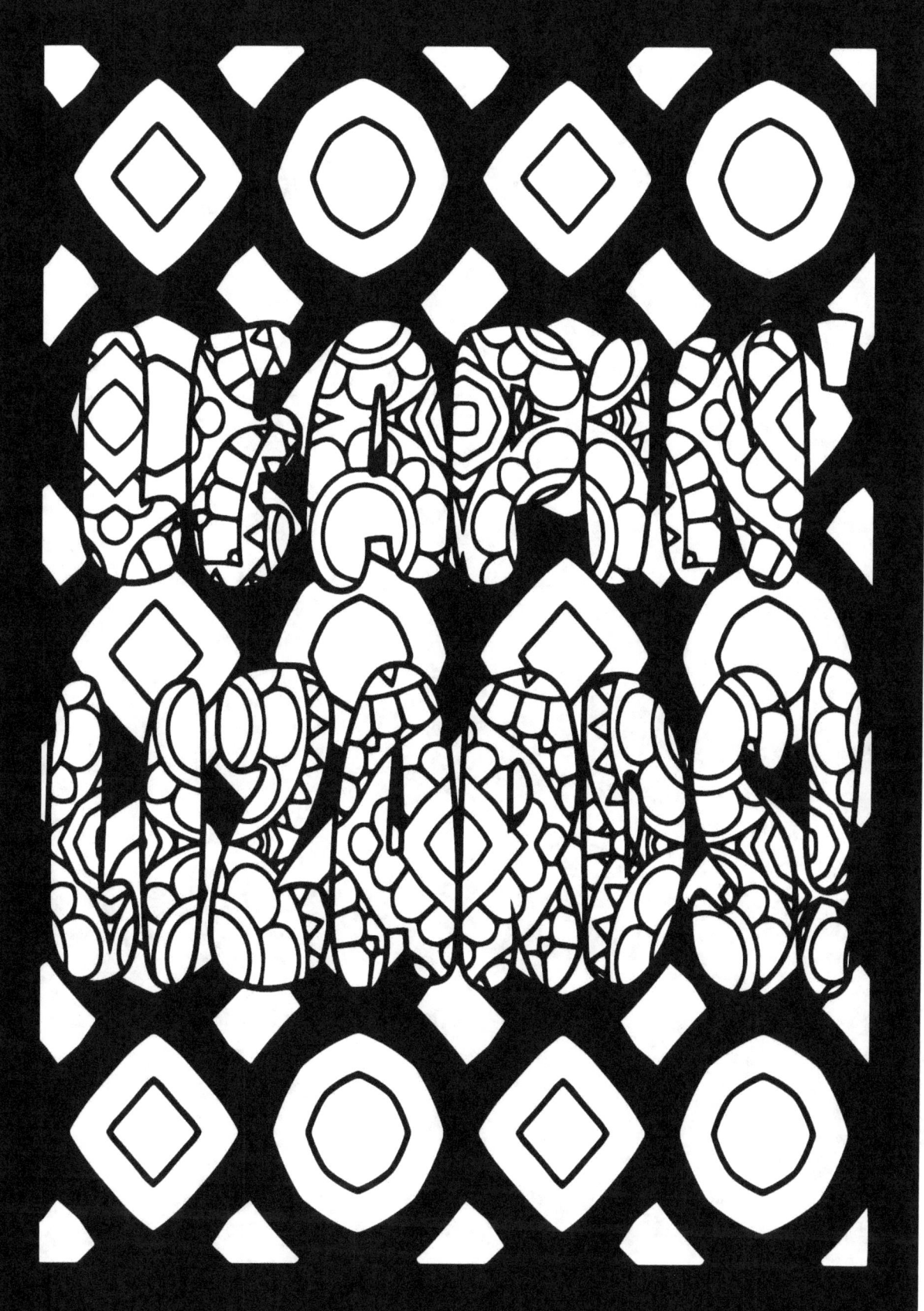

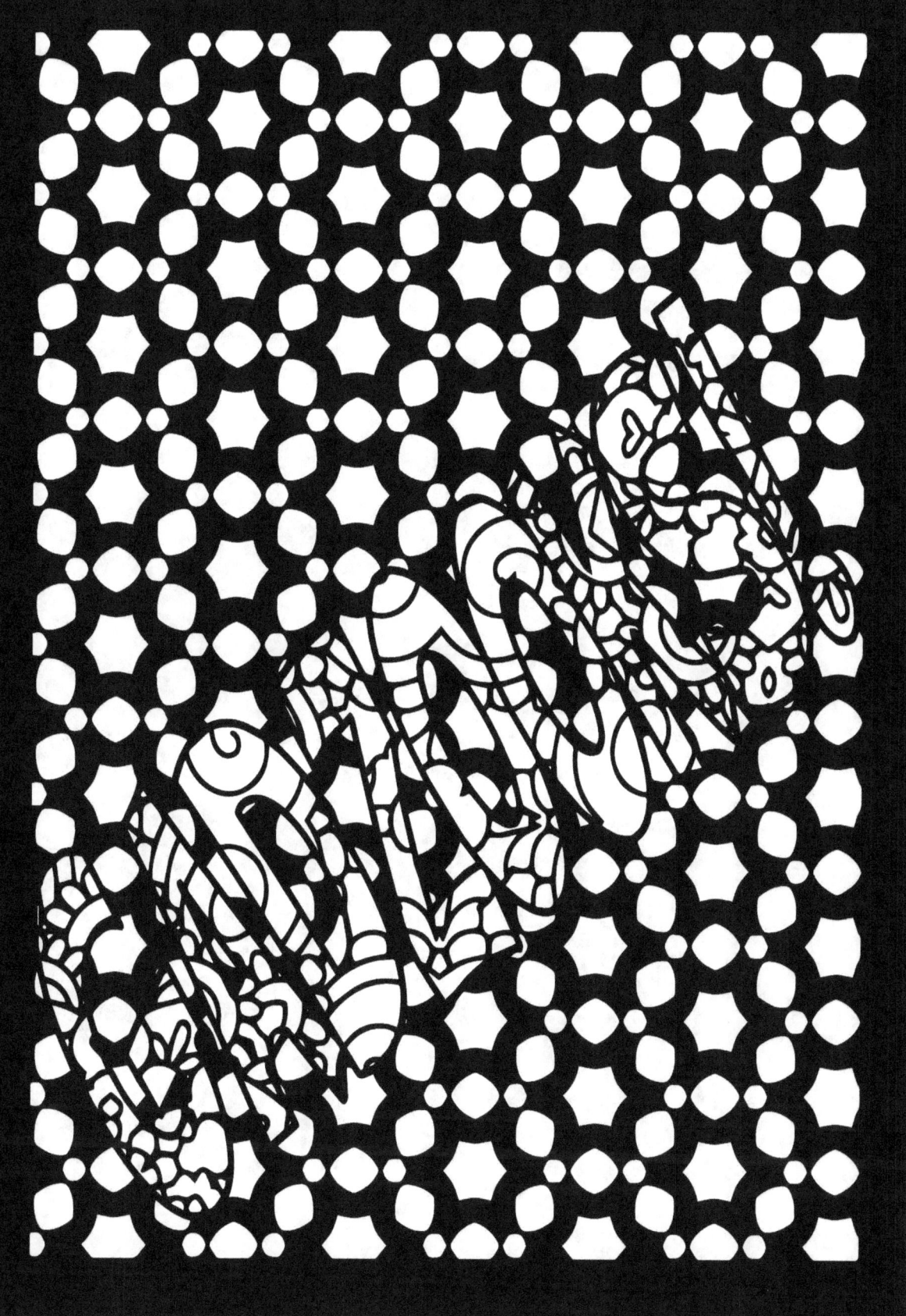

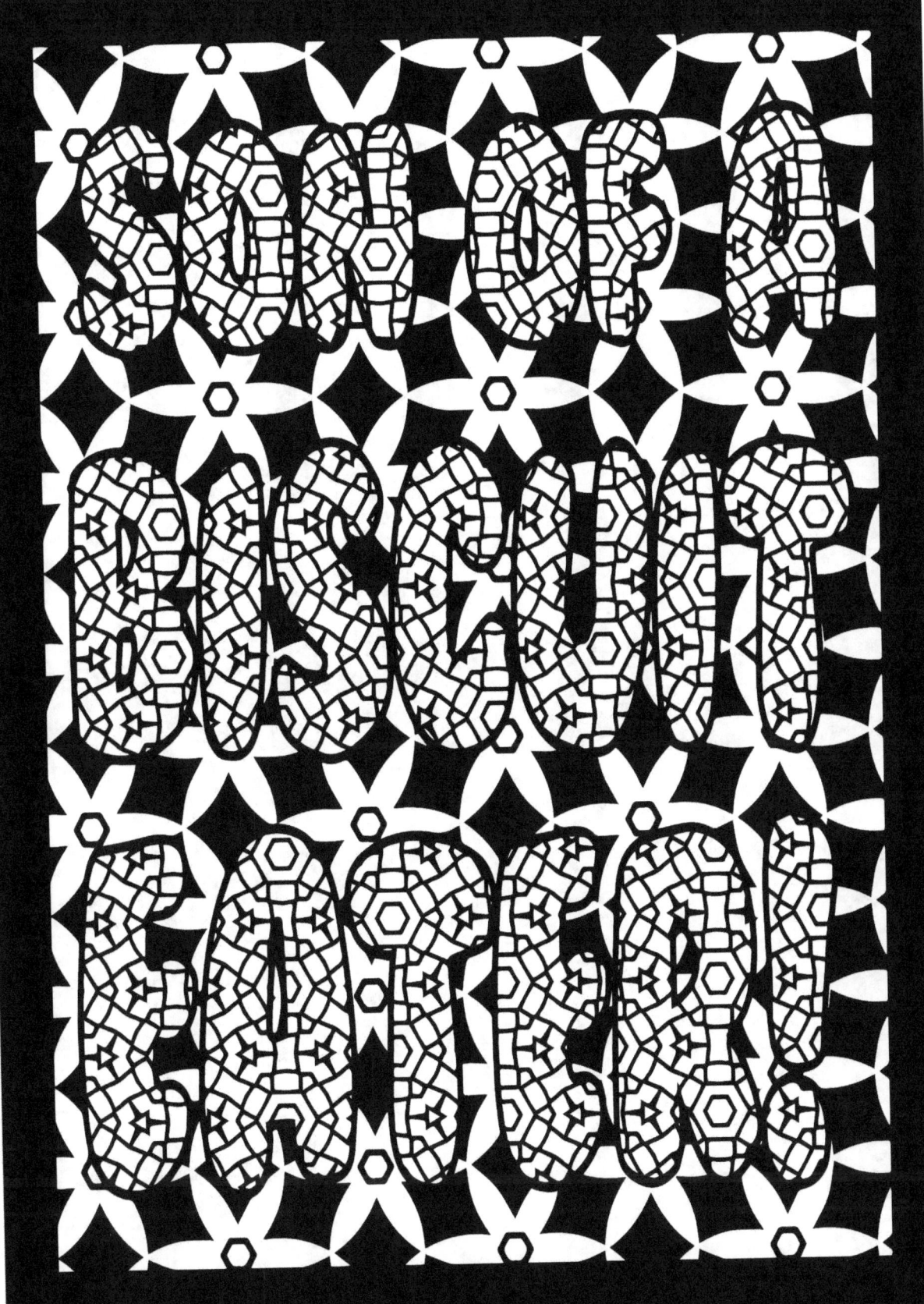

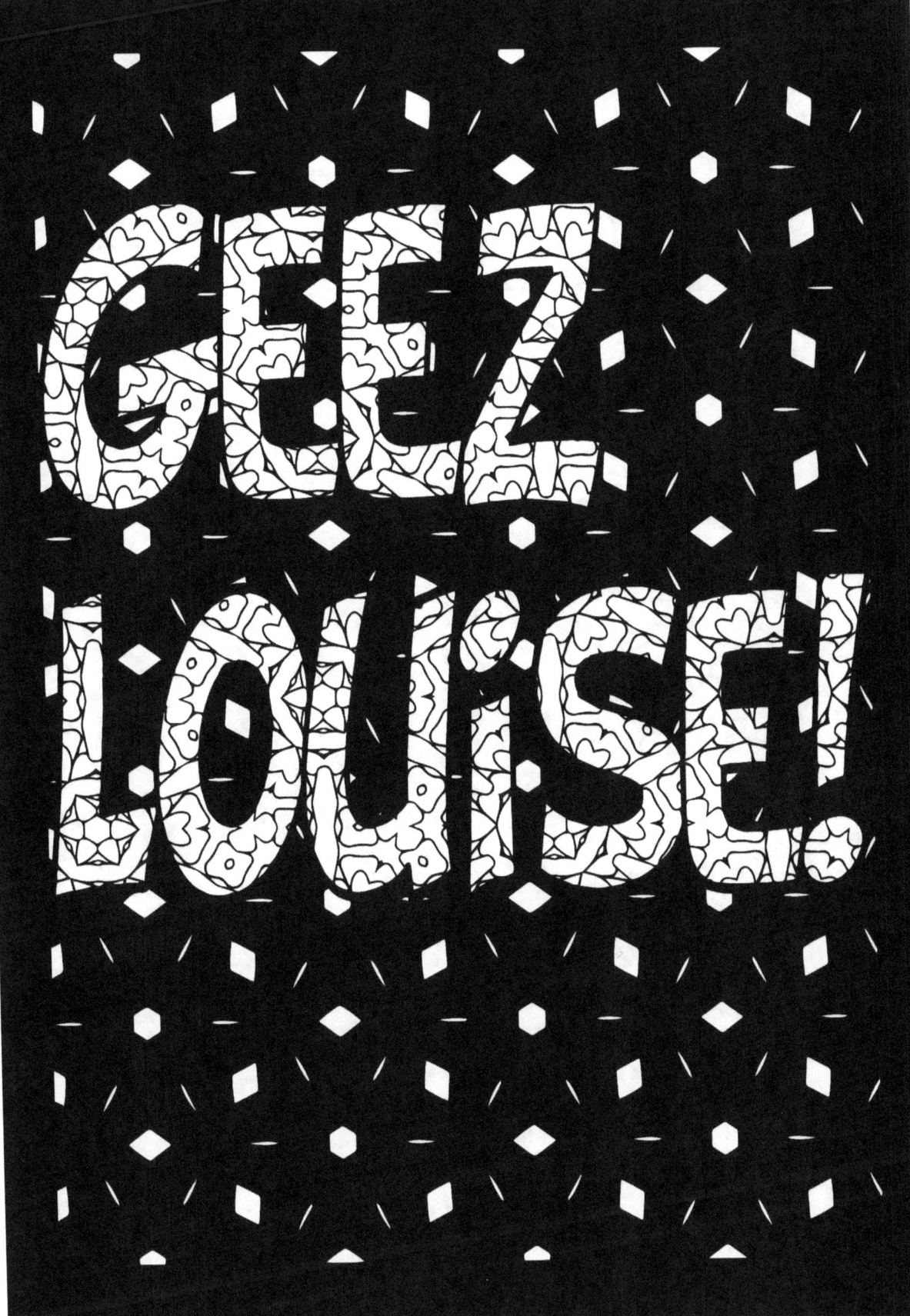

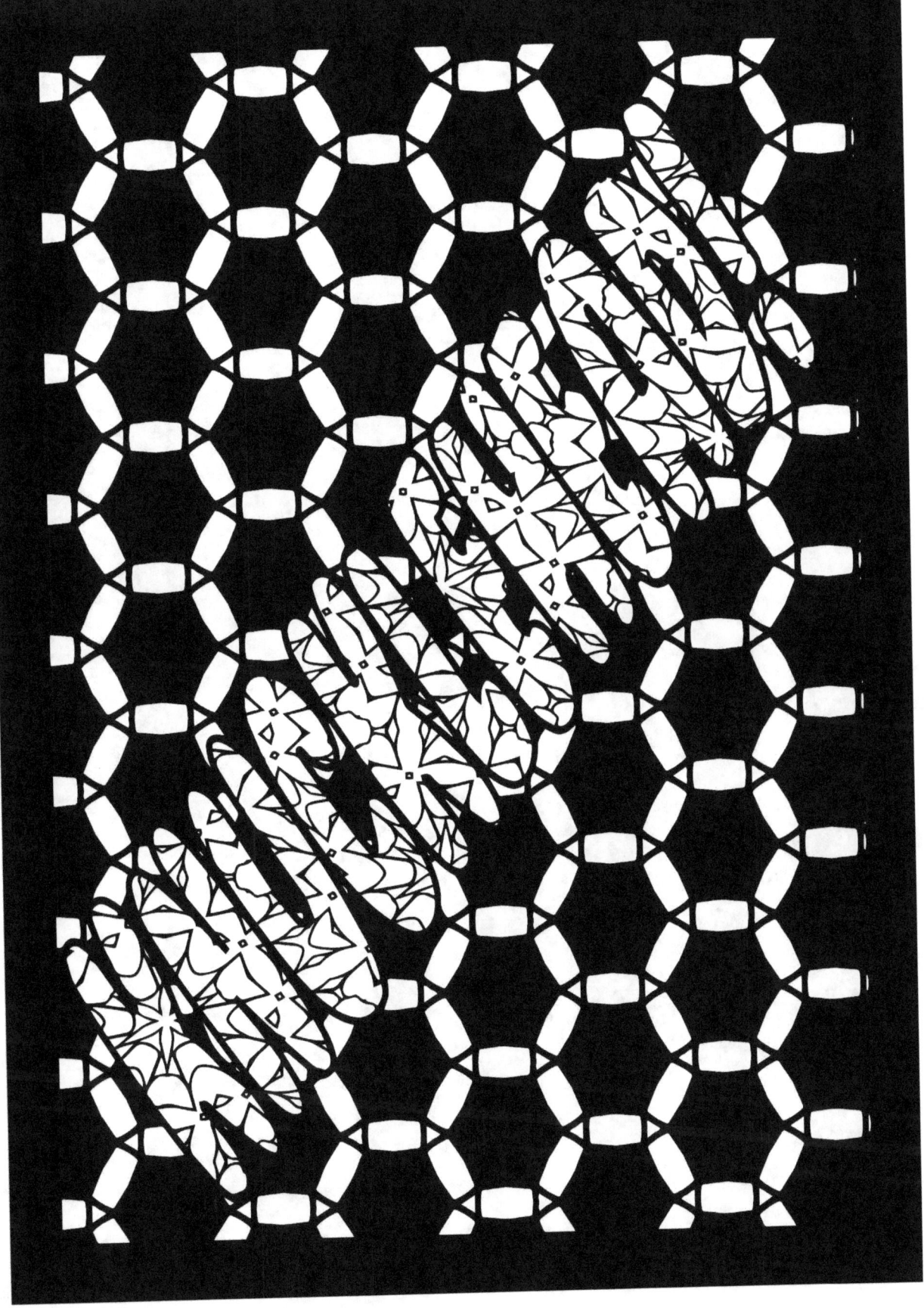

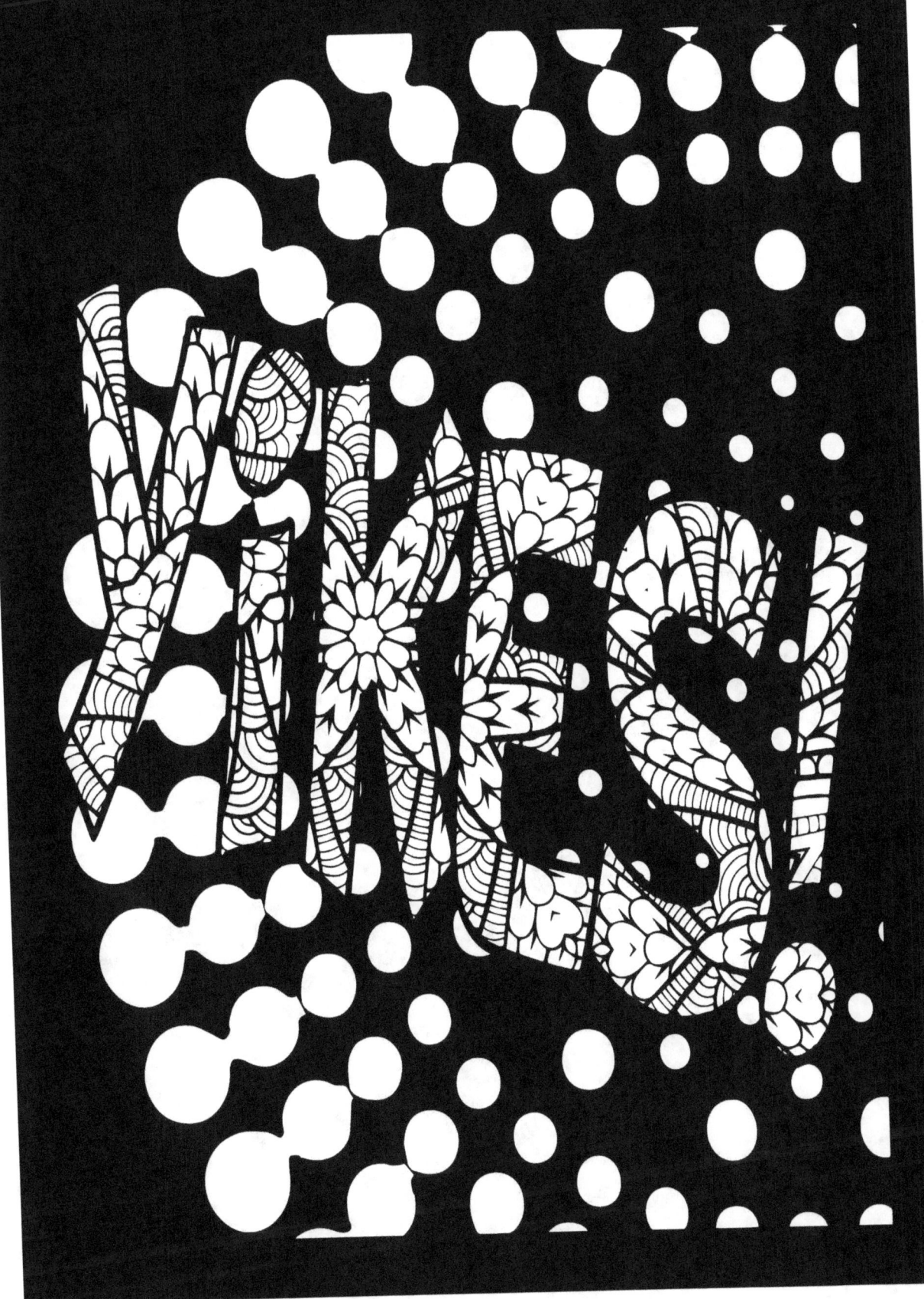

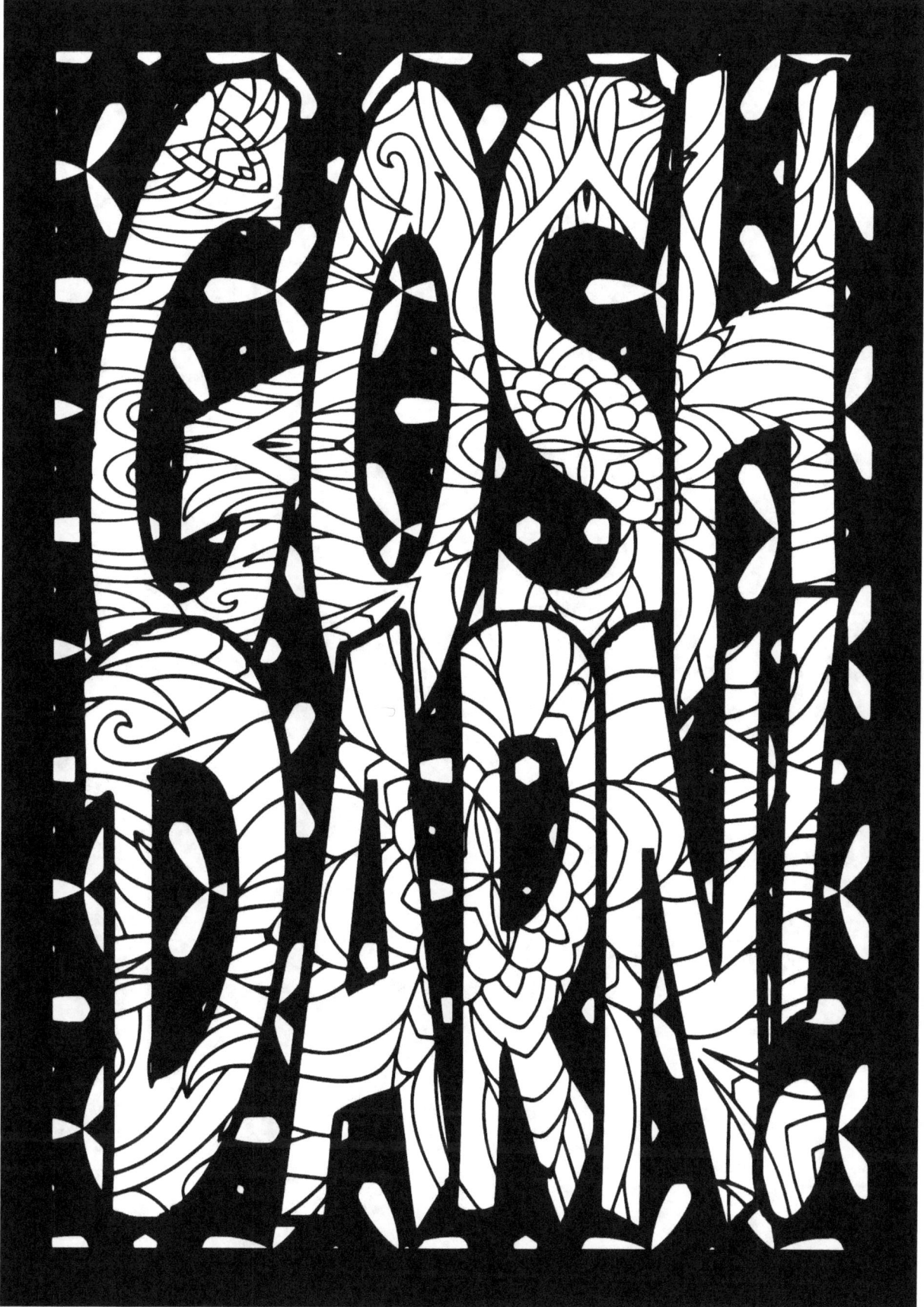

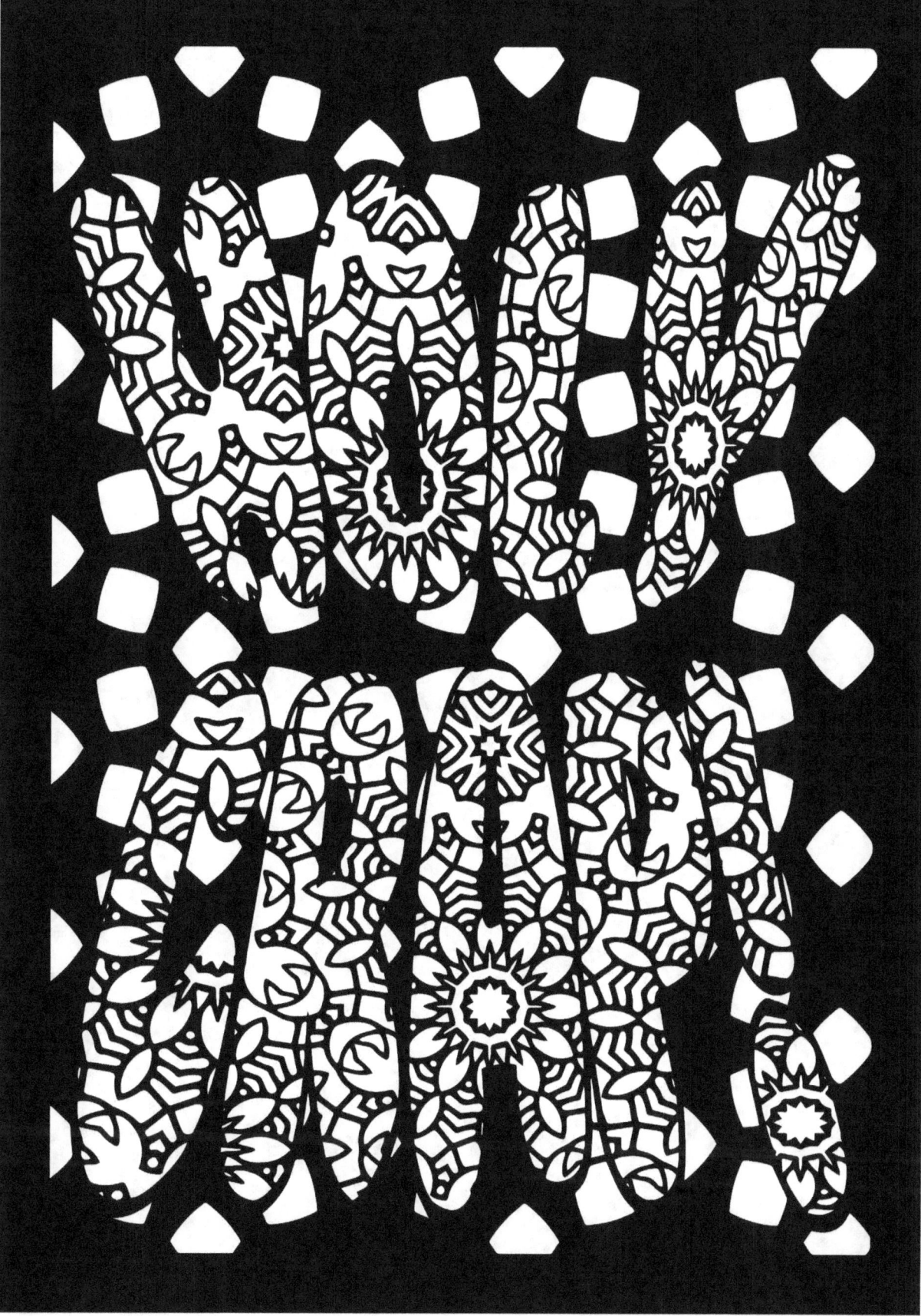

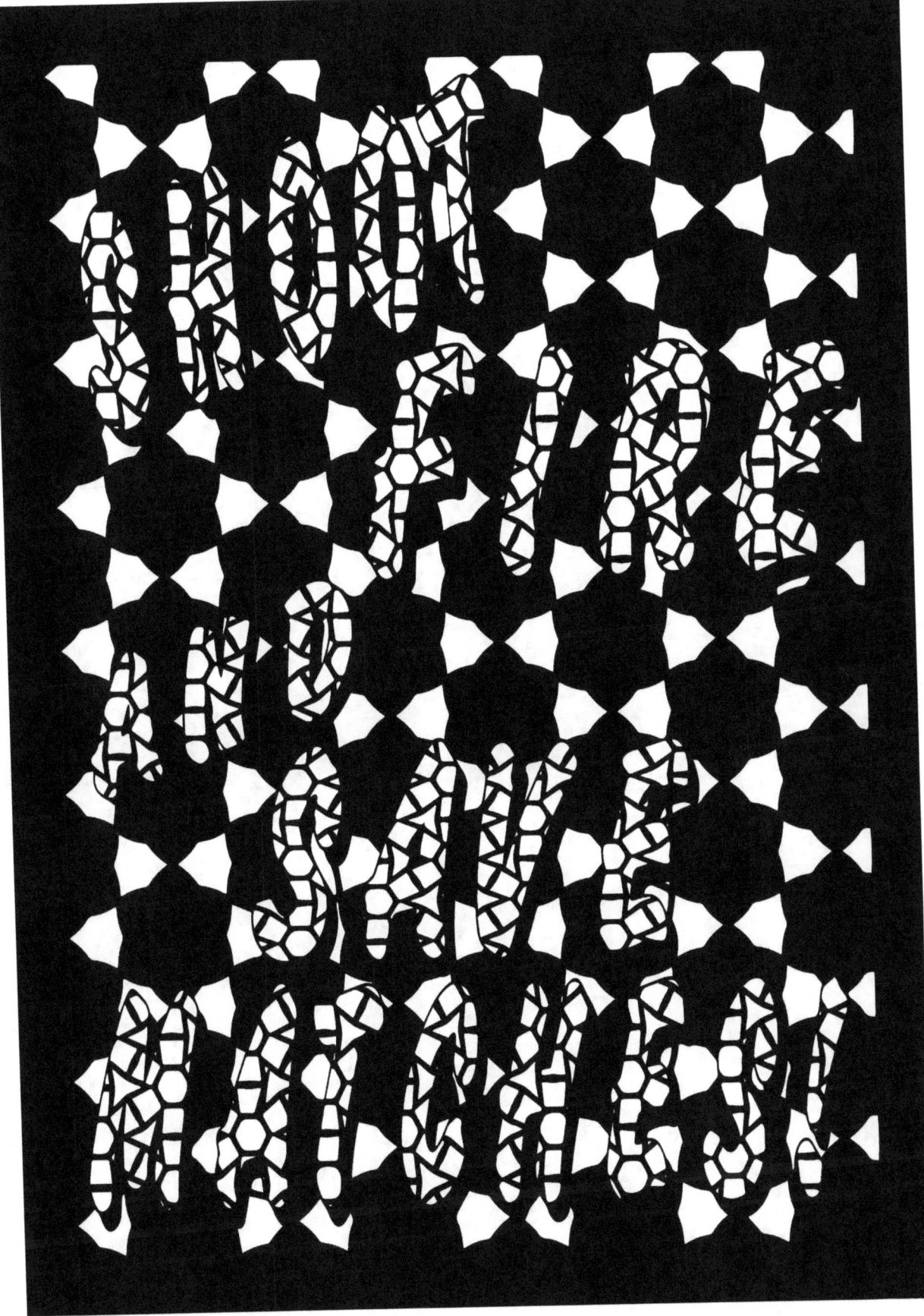

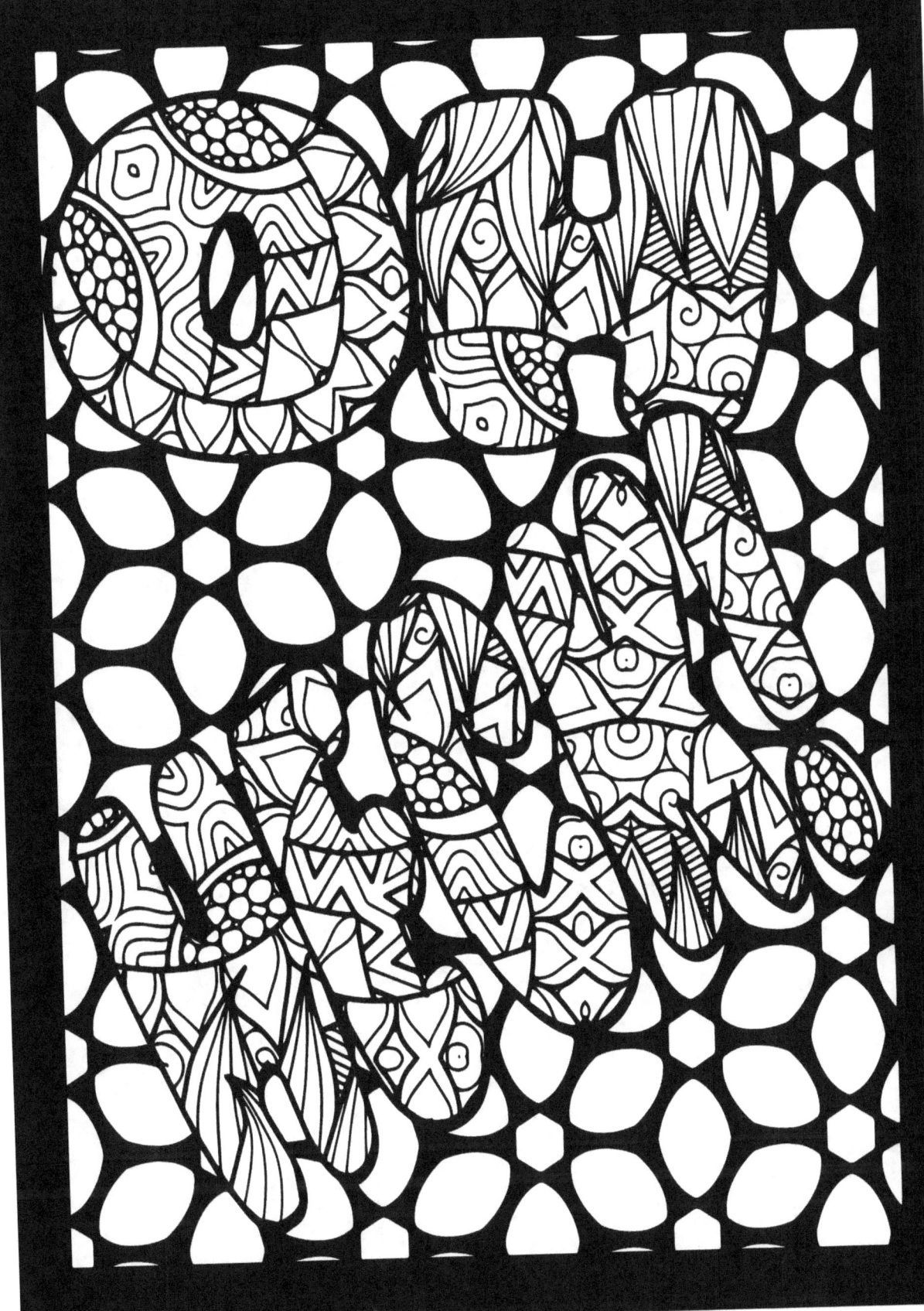

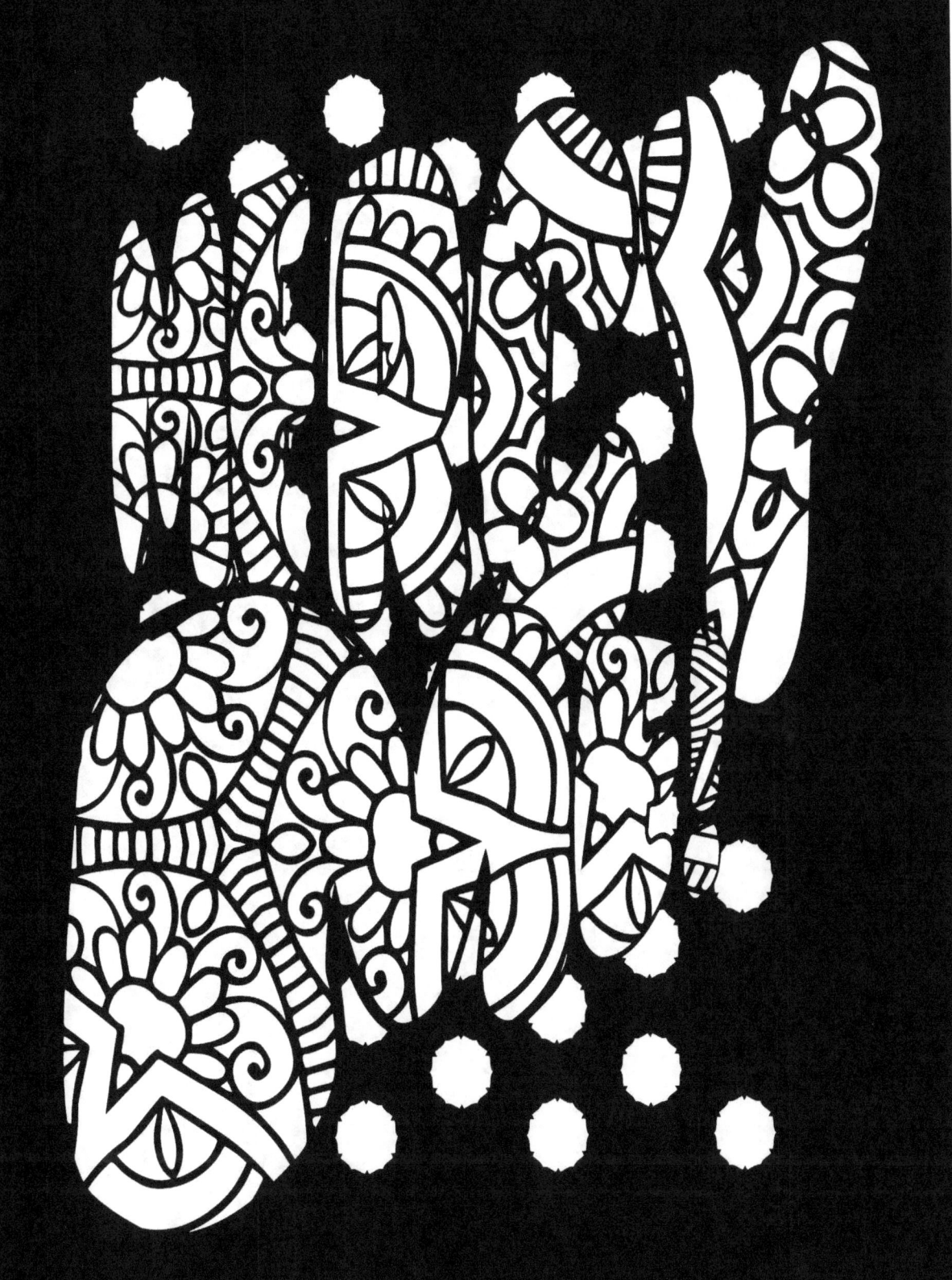

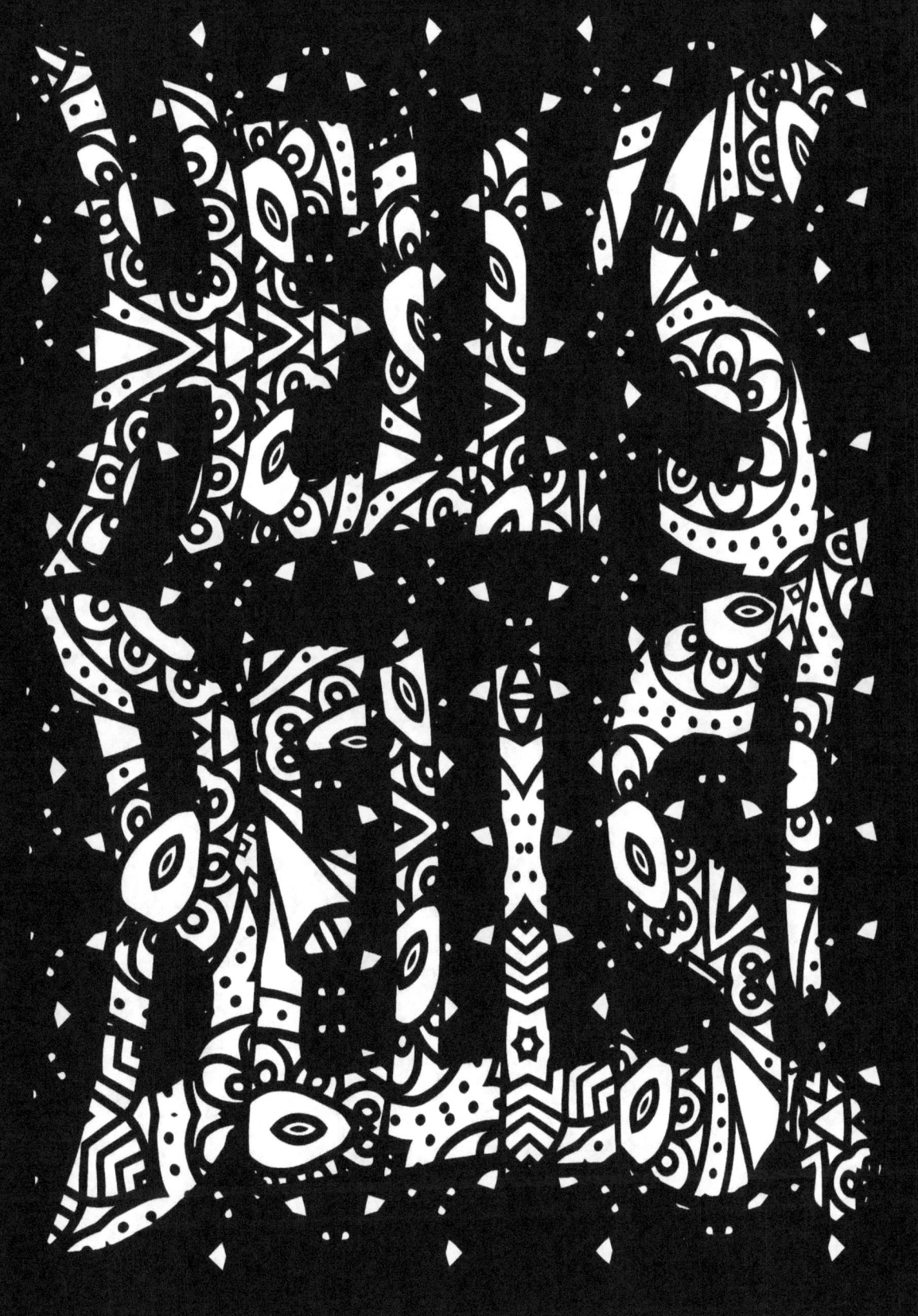

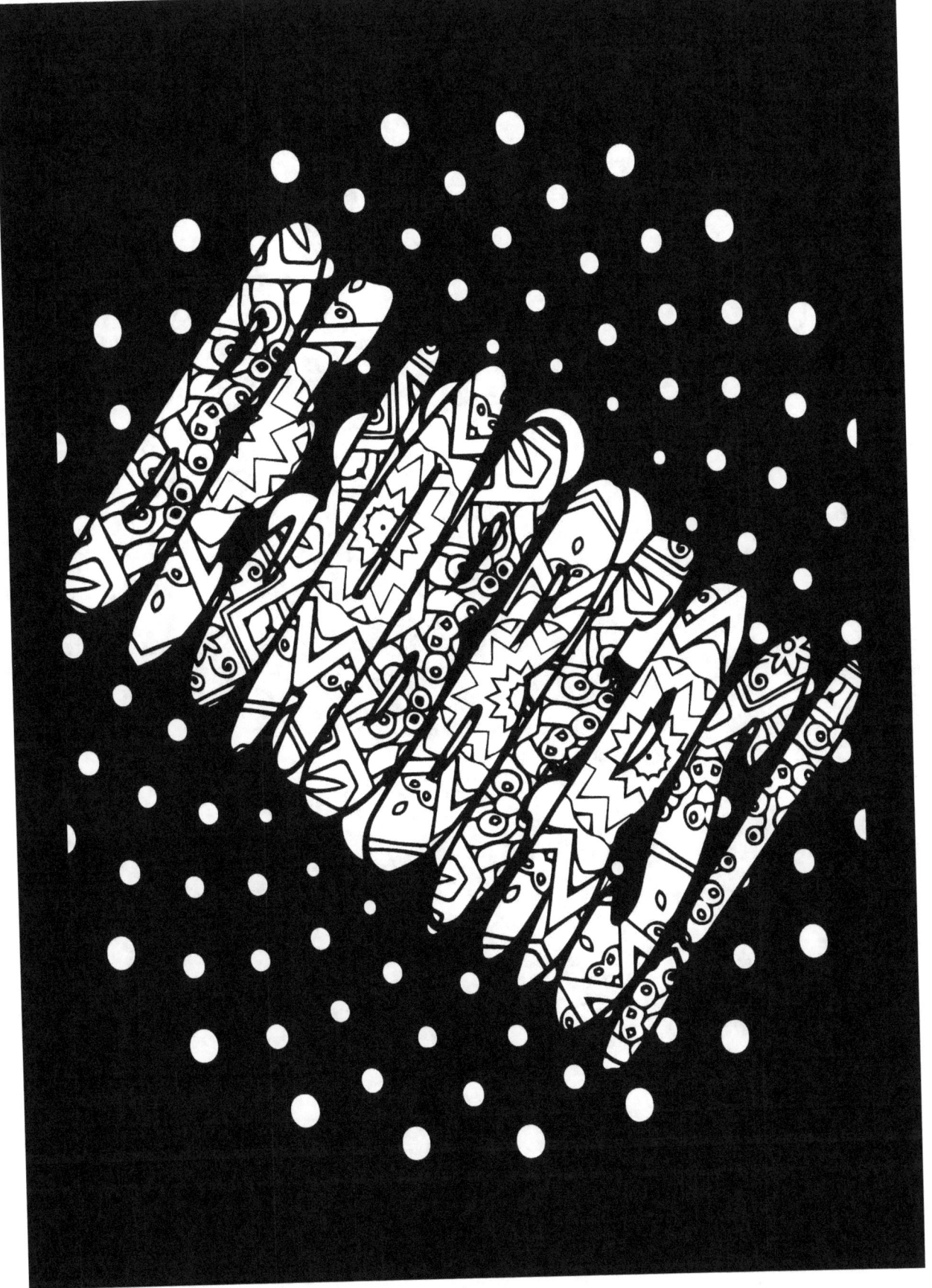

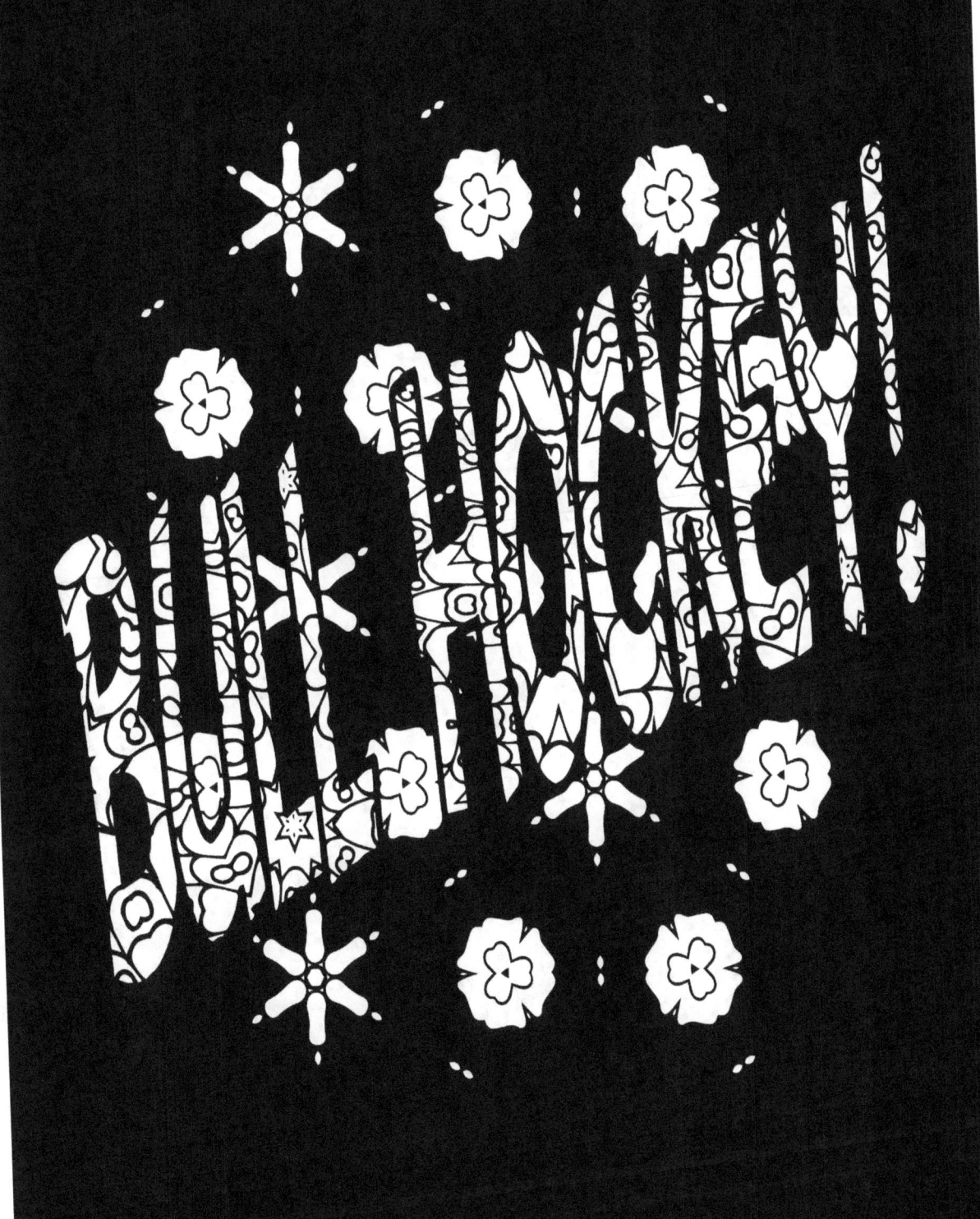

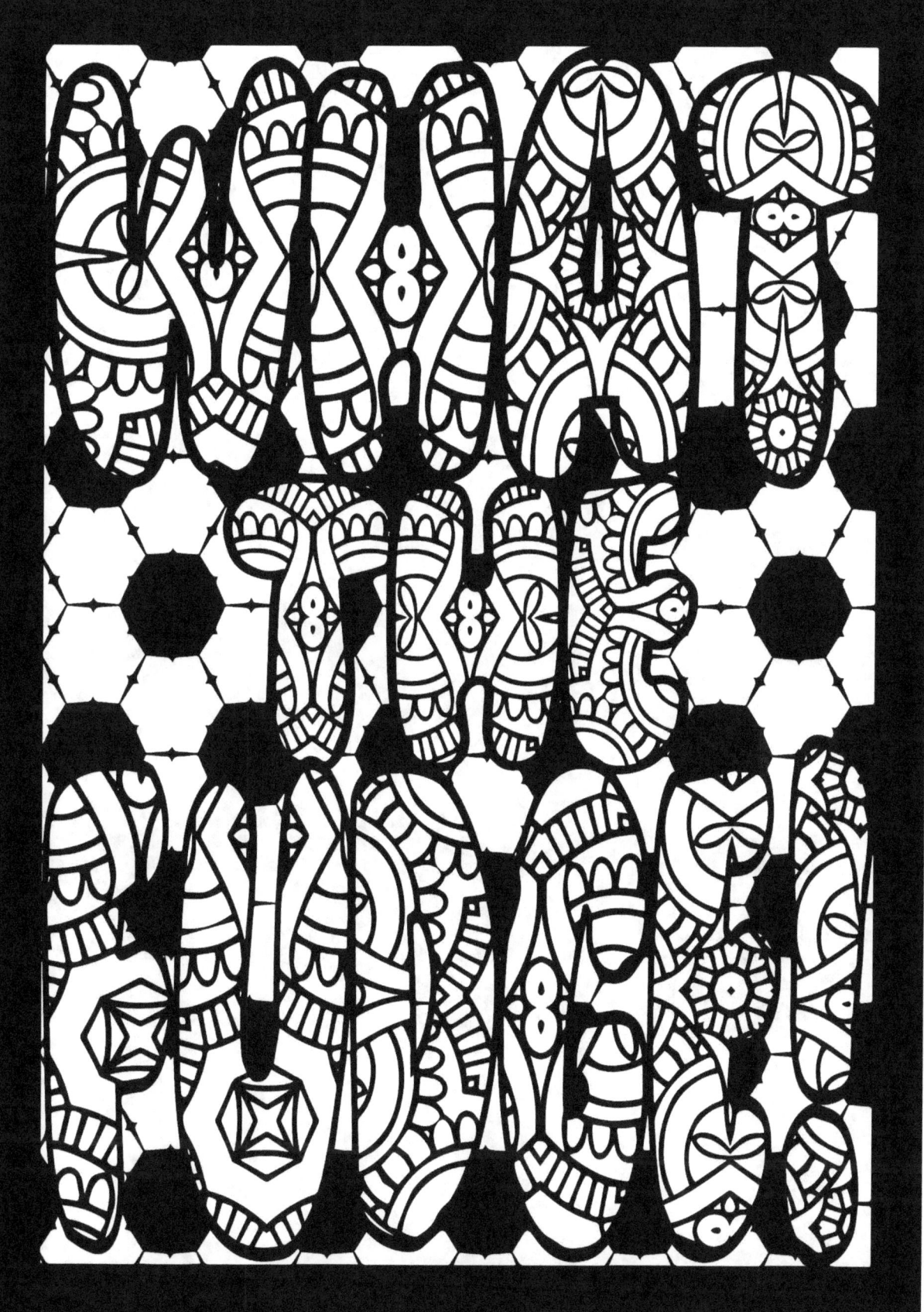

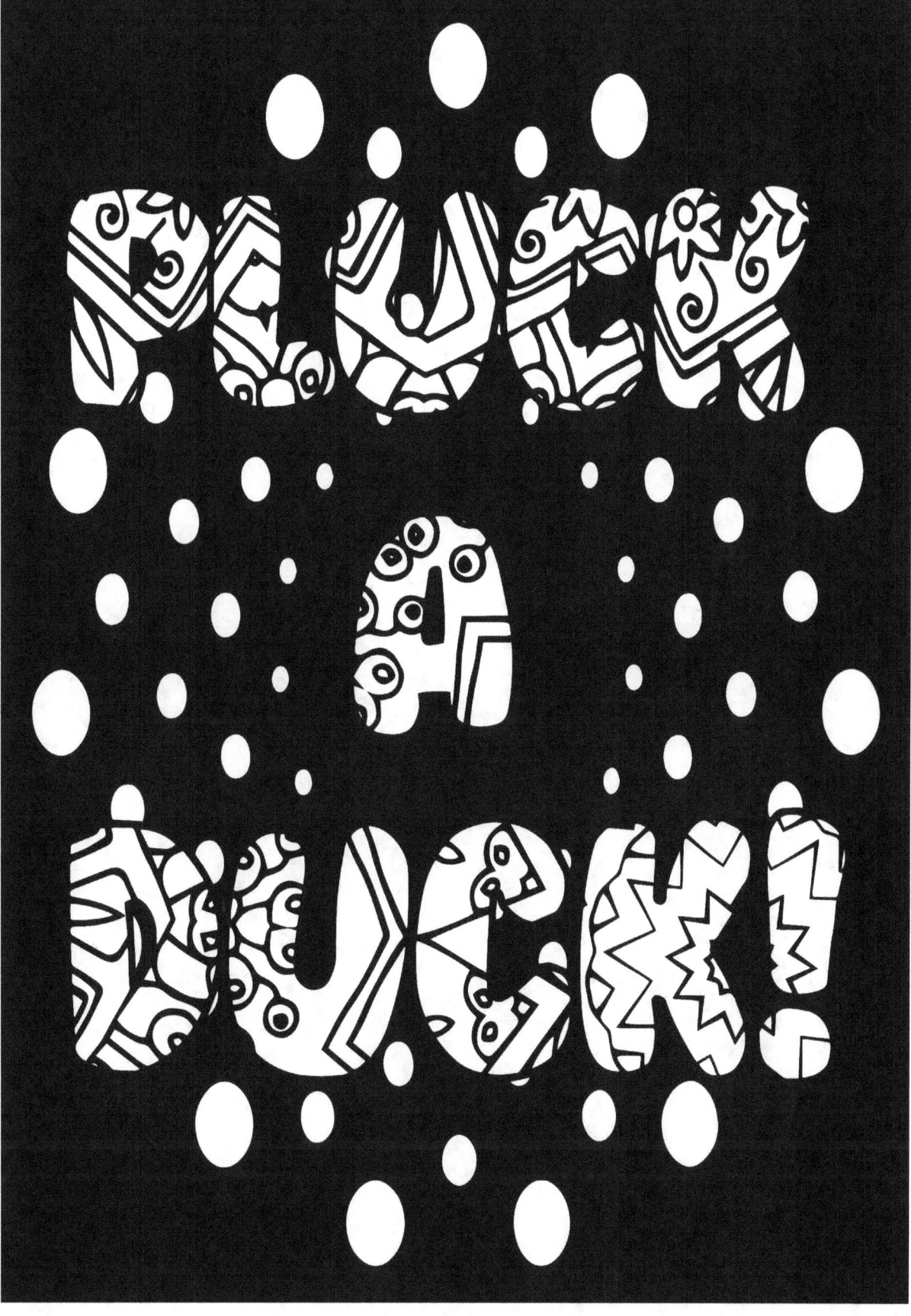

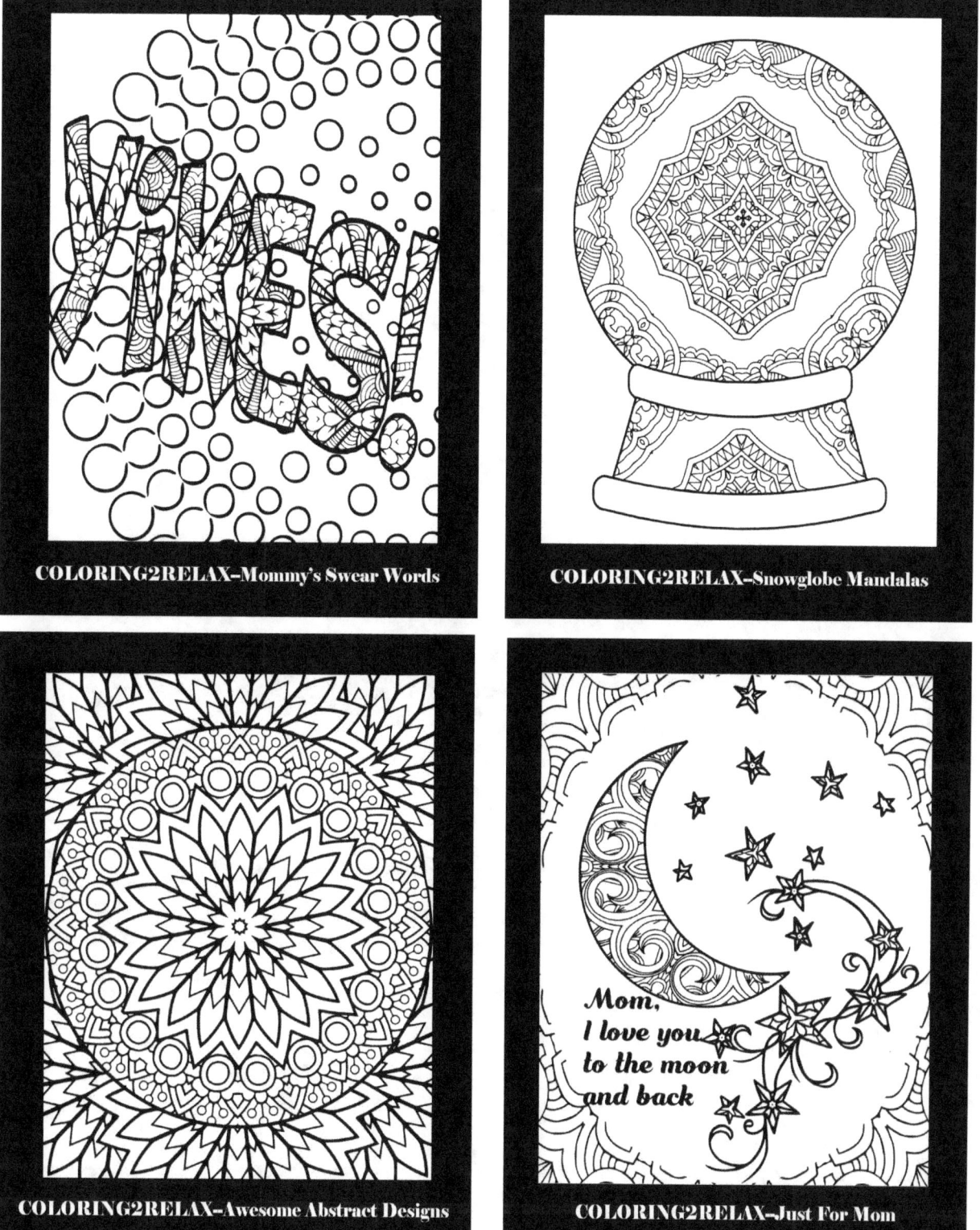

Samples of coloring pages from some of our most popular Adult Coloring Books
Visit our website, www.coloring2relax.com, to shop all of our products
Don't forget your 5 Free Coloring Pages while you are there!

Coloring Practice Page

Practice blending & Shading, try new colors, test markers & gel pens, decide on color palettes or add color palettes you want to use later

Coloring Practice Page

Practice blending & Shading, try new colors, test markers & gel pens, decide on color palettes or add color palettes you want to use later

Coloring Practice Page

Practice blending & Shading, try new colors, test markers & gel pens, decide on color palettes or add color palettes you want to use later

Coloring Practice Page

Practice blending & Shading, try new colors, test markers & gel pens, decide on color palettes or add color palettes you want to use later

Blank Page

Pull out and use underneath the page you are coloring for extra protection against bleed through and denting

Blank Page

Pull out and use underneath the page you are coloring for extra protection against bleed through and denting

Blank Page

Pull out and use underneath the page you are coloring for extra protection against bleed through and denting

www.ingramcontent.com/pod-product-compliance
Lightning Source LLC
Chambersburg PA
CBHW081122180526
45170CB00008B/2960